LANCASHIRE HOTCH-POTCH

Illustrated and written by Bob Bond

Max Books

First published in the UK in 2023 by Max Books

A CIP catalogue record for this title is available from the British Library

ISBN: 978-1-9196389-1-1

Typeset and Design by Andrew Searle

MAX BOOKS
2 Newbold Way
Nantwich
CW5 7AX
Email: maxcricket@btinternet.com
www.max-books.co.uk

CONTENTS

ABOUT THE AUTHOR

Bob Bond was born in Southport, where he attended Art College during the 1950s. He then drew pages for children's comics for many years before moving to the south of England with his wife and sons, where he continued to work as an illustrator for a Christian organisation. Although exiled, Bob continues to follow Preston North End. Consequently he looks older than he really is. As you can see from this book, he also follows Lancashire cricket. He was only a very ordinary cricketer himself, but enjoyed playing for local teams until he was well past his sell-by date. He has been a lay preacher, a youth worker and a Sunday School teacher, and continues to be active in the church. Bob also suffers from a huge inferiority complex because one of his sons is a much better artist than he is.

He has illustrated a few books on football:
'Both Legs Down One Knicker' published by Austin Macauley (autobiographical)
'Home of English Football' - a cartoon history of Wembley Stadium (Pitch Publishing)
Also club histories of Liverpool, Arsenal, Spurs and Manchester United.

FOREWORD

By David Lloyd

I've never been a big reader of books, let alone cricket books… and I have hundreds!
I collect 'em but don't read 'em.

But I do like picture books. As a lad I used to read comics… Topper, Beazer, Dandy, Beano … I liked to chuckle at the characters.

Bob's book caught my attention. I'm a lifelong Lancs lad… played a bit, coached a bit, talked a bit.

The characters he portrays are exactly as I saw them…. True Lancastrians, and all with different characters and characteristics.

I'm back to my comics. Bob's book made me chuckle. Memories, poignancy, nostalgia and fun.

What more do you want! Dig in!

INTRODUCTION

You've got to love Lancs...

You have to be interested in cricket, and particularly in Lancashire cricket, to get even a little bit of enjoyment from these pages. It might jog a few memories.

'Oh yes,' you might say, 'I was there that day. But that's not how I remember it...'

I confess that some of the comments and captions may have been used more than once. 'Have I used this one before?' Most cartoonists can't recall what they drew ten days ago, let alone ten years ago...

It's not really a book of statistics, although you might find the occasional batting average or bowling analysis has crept in unawares. But if you want stats, then go to your nearest bookstore and purchase a complete set of Wisden Cricketers' Almanacks. You should get them reasonably cheaply, as they are very old and almost certainly secondhand.

It's only a dip into Lancashire's colourful history. Nearly all of the memories are from before the Millennium. Even so, some important people in the Red Rose story have been left out, but not purposely. Nothing about Charlie Hallows, Len Hopwood or Jack Iddon, all prolific runscorers. No mention of Bob Entwistle or scores of other colourful characters. Glaring omissions. I know, but that's the way life is.

Another confession is that many of the match cartoons have been drawn in retro. Only a few were drawn at the time of the event.

If you've got this far without being bored, carry on and enjoy...

DAYS WATCHING LANCASHIRE

*'Flintoff, Lloyd and Engineer
Lanky Lanky Lankyshire!'*

The COUNTY CHAMPIONSHIP

77 years of hurt! COUNTY CHAMPIONS five times in nine years between the wars, Lancashire had to wait until 2011 before once again finishing top of the pile. So 2011 will live long in the memory of Lancashire followers, and Simon Kerrigan and Gary Keedy both had their days and moments which contributed greatly to that Championship success. Keedy's throw to run out the last Somerset batsman on the very final day... the following cartoon remembers that brilliant spin bowling by Kerrigan at Aigburth.

...and then a reminder of that famous day at Taunton.

...But in cricket, as in the stock market, past results are no guarantee of future performance. In 2012, the summer following their title win, Lancashire fell down with a bump, relegated...

BUXTON was never an easy place to go to. Older Lancashire followers will remember waking up to the dreadful news, not long after the war, that their county had closed the second day on four runs for four wickets. This snow-interrupted match was in 1975...

It was at Blackpool in 1959 that Jim Stewart of Warwickshire broke the six-hitting record with 17 in the match. Jim, a magnificent striker, reportedly went into his shell later in his career and refused to entertain the crowds anymore. There's nowt as strange as cricketers...

Southport! It's not in the south, and it's not a port. There is a pier and a broad expanse of sand, but the sea hardly ever comes close.

Southport's main attraction is Lord Street, with its wide pavements and glorious shops, behind wrought-iron canopies. A lesser claim to fame is the birth of the 'Eagle' comic here in the 1950s. It's where Frank Hampson did his first drawings of 'Dan Dare - Pilot of the Future'. Inspired by Frank's story and being from the same town, the artist of this book from an early age wanted to 'draw comics'.

Southport has an attractive little cricket ground, with the train running alongside, and many a six has been clobbered on to or over the tracks.

It was here, in the 1980s, that Alvin Kallicharran and Geoff Humpage put on 470 runs for Warwickshire on the first day of a county match. They could have reached 1000, but kindly declared at 500+... In face of such a score, Lancashire's only hope would be to bat for a draw, wouldn't it? Batting with a runner, 'Foxy' Fowler hit a century on the second day.

Here's a cartoon of day three...

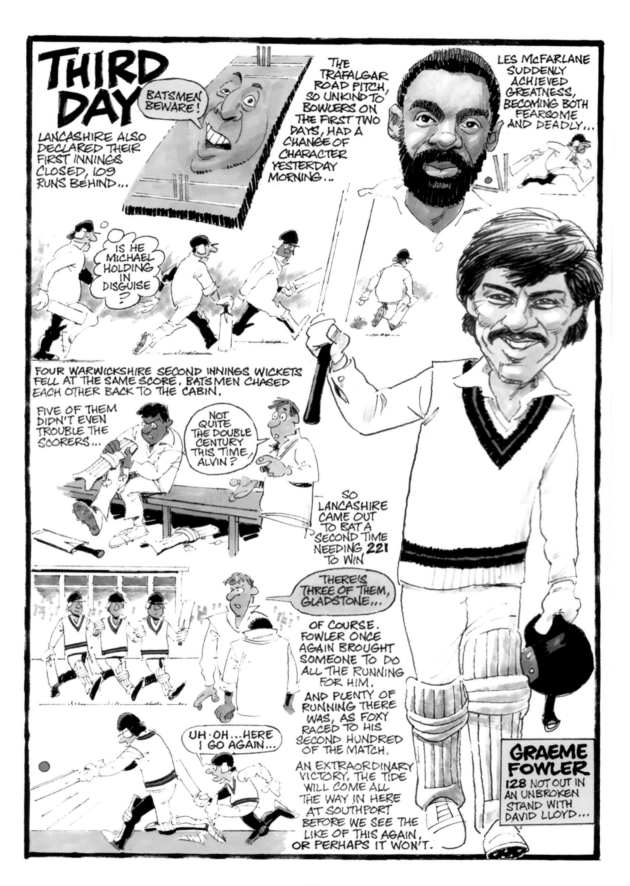

It's simply not true to say that only one good thing comes out of YORKSHIRE and that is the road to Lancashire. Barry Wood, for example.In recent years a visit to Leeds by Lancashire has been likened to a trip to Galatasaray. We all know what that means.

'Welcome to Hell...'

In fact cricket followers everywhere have had to admire and be jealous of the White Rose for all those County Championships won. And all those superstars. But here are a couple of occasions in the County Championship when the Red Rose has been triumphant....The first, in 1924, was immortalised by Neville Cardus in one of his inimitable essays...

...Then a game from 1950 when Lancashire were almost County Champions, but had to share the title with Surrey.

The GILLETTE CUP

Lancashire were NOT the first winners of the Gillette Cup. In fact it took them eight years to get their hands on the trophy, although PETER MARNER was the first centurian in the competition in 1963. Having won it once, they did their best to keep it forever. It was a 65 overs a side job in those early days. The following pages celebrate some of Lancashire's famous victories in this inaugural one day competition.

Uncle JACK BOND came into a struggling Lancashire team in the 1960s, and advanced to become a great leader. They looked around for a captain to replace the retiring Brian Statham, and there he was...

Here's a reminder of those three consecutive triumphs, not forgetting Bond's famous catch in the 1971 final...

GILLETTE CUP SEMI FINAL

IS THAT THEE, SKIPPER?

IF THA CAN SEE IT, 'IT IT...

SOME PEOPLE ARE GOOD TO HAVE IN THE TEAM WHEN DARKNESS CLOSES IN.

SUCH A MAN IS **DAVID HUGHES**, WHO WAS MAN OF THE MATCH AT OLD TRAFFORD LAST EVENING...

FOR EVENING IT WAS WHEN HUGHES MARCHED OUT TO THE WICKET. LANCASHIRE SKIPPER JACK BOND HAD ALREADY CHOSEN TO BAT ON IN THE FAST ENCIRCLING GLOOM.

DICKY WASN'T HAPPY, BUT DICKY NEVER IS...

ONE DAY THEY'LL GIVE US SOME KIND OF LIGHT METER, SO WE'LL KNOW WHEN IT'S TOO DARK TO PLAY...

HUGHES SAW ENOUGH OF THE BALL TO HIT IT...

JOHN MORTIMORE WAS THE BOWLER HE TOOK A LIKING TO...

UH-OH...

24 FROM ONE OVER WAS ROUGHER TREATMENT THAN MORTY DESERVED.

HE SPENT SOME TIME GAZING SKYWARDS AS THE BALL SAILED AWAY.

HAVE SOME OF THAT...

HUGHES WAS CAUGHT TWICE.

BY A SPECTATOR

YOURS ARTHUR!

DARK? I CAN SEE ALL REET...

LANKY FANS WENT HOME HAPPY TO BE IN ANOTHER FINAL...

IT ALL FINISHED AT TEN MINUTES TO NINE. BY WHICH TIME DICKY COULDN'T SEE HIS WAY BACK TO THE PAVILION.

COME 'ERE, LUV. DID I EVER TELL YOU HOW MUCH YOU REMIND ME OF FLAT JACK?

Just before, there was that famous evening in July 1971 when Lancashire defeated Gloucestershire at nine o'clock in the evening. 'I know, 'cos I was there!' was Max Boyce's well known claim. 'And sometimes you said it when you wasn't there!' Fifty thousand people insist they were there on that evening. And even if you wasn't there you must have caught the ending live on television. When some of the players complained that they couldn't see, umpire Arthur Jepson pointed to the sky and said 'Can you see the moon? How much further do you want to see?'

No, Jack wasn't related to the artist at all. It simply felt to every Lancastrian that he was their favourite uncle at that time. For, until he pulled down that catch, Asif was winning the game for Kent.

Here, too, CLIVE LLOYD's match winning hundred in the 1972 Gillette Final. Just one of many memorable innings by the West Indian favourite...

And a popular win over Yorkshire, who at that time were not quite so effective in this one day game as they were in the longer County Championship format.

GILLETTE CUP FINAL

MIDDLESEX WERE 'AT HOME'...

...WELCOMING LANCASHIRE THE DISTANT NORTH.

ALSO FROM THE NORTH, BUT FROM THE OTHER SIDE OF THE PENNINES, CAME ONE OF THE UMPIRES, YOUNG MR BIRD...

HELLO... I'M A LITTLE DICKIE.

I'M NOT FEELING TOO GOOD MYSELF...

AS MIDDLESEX STRUGGLED TO 180, LANCASHIRE'S **BOB RATCLIFFE** HAD A GOOD DAY WITH THE BALL.

DAMN HAIR GOT INTO MY EYES...

LARRY GOMES GOT MORE THAN ANYONE, BUT BOB GOT ONE THROUGH HIS DEFENCE.

MR BIRD GAVE HIS DECISIONS WITH COMPLETE CERTAINTY.

AS I LIVE AND BREATHE, THAT'S **OUT**...

THE MEMBERS WERE NOT ALWAYS IN AGREEMENT...

I SAY UMPIRE — ARE YOU COMPLETELY SURE

WHOEVER FINDS IT, THROW IT BACK...

180 WAS NEVER ENOUGH WHEN CLIVE LLOYD GOT INTO HIS STRIDE, AND IT'S A BIG STRIDE HE HAS, HE NEARLY TREADS ON THE BOWLER'S TOES.

HE WAS SOON LIFTING HIS BAT TO THE LANKY FANS, **73** NOT OUT.

SO LANCS WON WITH LOTS TO SPARE...

HOME SUPPORTERS WENT BACK TO THE LEAFY LANES OF MIDDLESEX, WONDERING IF THEY'D **EVER** WIN ANYTHING.

Lancashire's fourth Gillette Cup success in 1975 was their easiest so far. Clive Lloyd had already led the West Indies to victory in the first ever World Cup tournament earlier in the summer, hitting a century in the final at Lord's. Here he was, back at Headquarters, doing it again. And Man of the Match once more...

The Gillette Cup (other razor blades are available) later became the NATWEST CUP, and here are a few more of Lancashire's successful visits to Headquarters...

As you can see, it was the bowlers who had a big part to play. PHILIP DEFREITAS spoiled the 1990 final as a serious contest with an early spell of eight overs in which he knocked over five good batsmen.

GLENN CHAPPLE was even more destructive a few years later against Graham Gooch's Essex. Why was Chapple never chosen by England? Why is the sky so big?

And PETER MARTIN and IAN AUSTIN rolled over a weak Derbyshire team when it rained and the match had to go into a second day.

Then there was the BENSON AND HEDGES CUP, a slightly shorter one day competition which it took Lancashire a long time to win...This was not a final, but it was a remarkable match against Surrey at the Oval when Lancashire snatched a victory from the jaws of defeat.

Get your fingers crunched against the bat handle by a lifter from WASIM AKRAM and you'd never play the piano again. Wasn't Wasim good looking? Ladies swooned when he came out to bat or bowl or simply to blow his nose. Or to comb his hair, of which he had plenty (see also 'Haircuts'). But his handsome appearance belied a mean streak. He bowled lightning bolts at you with his left arm. Didn't you just love Wasim when he helped to bowl England out in the World Cup Final in 1992? Okay, no you didn't. But playing for Lancashire, such destruction of the foe was perfectly fine. Bless the day when Wasim first pulled on the sweater with the red rose.

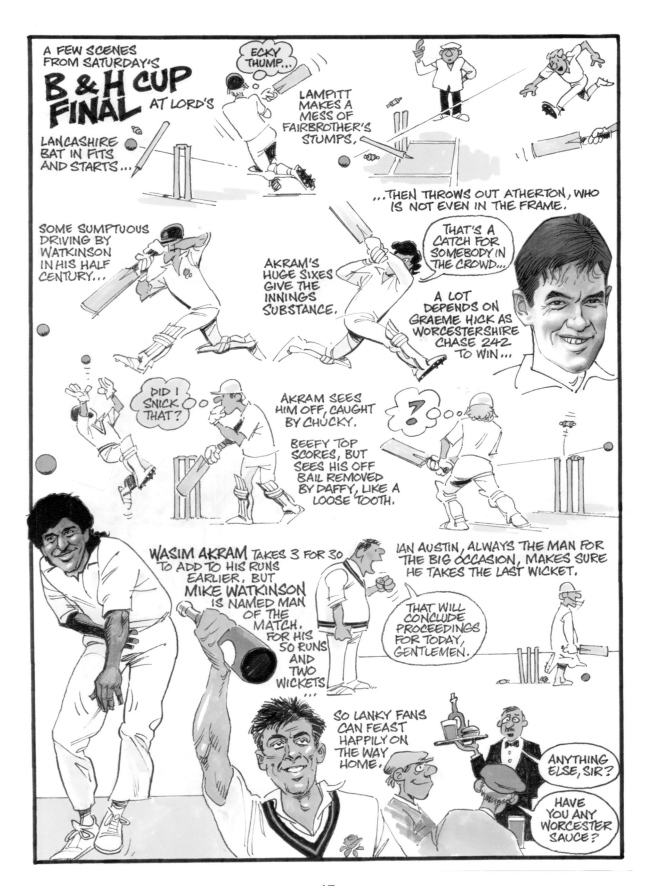

B&H FINAL

AT LORD'S... KENT v LANCASHIRE.

LANKY... LANKY... LANKY... LANKY... LANKY-SHEEER!

IT'S A FAMILIAR REFRAIN TO BE HEARD IN THIS PART OF OUR CAPITAL CITY AT THIS TIME OF YEAR AS THESE SUMMER MIGRANTS GET READY TO FLY OFF TO THEIR NORMAL WINTER HABITATS OF EWOOD PARK OR GIGG LANE, LANCASHIRE LOST SEVEN WICKETS IN MAKING 274...

LOOK FOR FIVE...

FIELD WHERE YOU WANT TO. I'M BOWLING FOR RUN OUTS...

WHEN ATHERTON AND CRAWLEY WERE BATTING TOGETHER, KENT WERE BOWLING MORE IN HOPE... ...THAN EXPECTATION

MIKE ATHERTON COULD SEE THE PROMISED LAND OF A CENTURY, BUT JUST FAILED TO GET THERE

JOHN CRAWLEY MADE 83...

IS IT SOMETHING I SAID?

LANCASHIRE'S SCORE WAS A FEW TOO MANY FOR KENT. DE SILVA PLAYED THE BEST INNINGS OF THE DAY, BUT COULDN'T FIND ANYONE TO STAY WITH HIM.

GARY YATES LEFT HIS WINE LODGE LONG ENOUGH TO TAKE THREE WICKETS FOR 42 IN ELEVEN TIGHT OVERS.

MIKE WATKINSON PROUDLY ACCEPTED THE GOLD TROPHY ON BEHALF OF HIS TEAM.

LLOYD FINALLY CAUGHT DE SILVA OFF WATKINSON, AND THE SRI LANKAN GOT A GREAT OVATION FOR HIS FINE INNINGS.

IS 112 STILL NOT ENOUGH?

WITH HIM GONE, KENT WERE ALL GONE,

AS GOOD AS.

LANCS WON BY 35 RUNS.

B&H CUP

We all love MICHAEL ATHERTON, don't we? We loved him when he batted on and on and on for England in ... in 1995, securing a draw in a Test Match that seemed lost. Ten hours and more, undefeated, breaking South African hearts. We watched in horror when he slipped, and was run out for 99 by Australia's Merv Hughes. We scratched our heads at his momentary fall from grace when fiddling around in his trousers for some dirt with which to do some tampering. And don't we just love his words of wisdom from the commentary box, from where it is always easier to play the bowling. Michael is Lancashire through and through. And JOHN CRAWLEY made batting look so easy. One couldn't help the feeling that he underachieved for England. A hundred by Crawley contained all the shots played to absolute perfection. Here they both are playing for their beloved County in a one day B and H final... But you had to feel sorry for Aravinda de Silva, who made such a delightful century.

The JOHN PLAYER LEAGUE

'It's cricket, Jim, but not as we know it...' The advent of the JOHN PLAYER LEAGUE in 1969 took some of the counties by surprise, but Lancashire seemed better prepared than any of them to embrace it. In Clive Lloyd and Farokh Engineer they had just the overseas players to drive the bus, and Harry Pilling was a pint of umbrage in a teacup. Lancashire won it the first year, and then underlined their dominance by winning it again. The followers, too, loved this form of the game and flooded back through the turnstiles.

Glamorgan won the County Championship in 1969, but this is FAROKH ENGINEER taking them apart in a Sunday League match in Southport that year.

And here's a match against the old enemy the following year...

The REFUGE ASSURANCE LEAGUE

'Cometh the hour, cometh the man...' It's an often repeated phrase in sport... and at this particular hour it was Paul Allott who answered Lancashire's call to arms. Paul was better known for his bowling, but could give the ball a mighty biff when required to. Did he not get a fifty in his first Test innings? To win the REFUGE ASSURANCE LEAGUE in 1989 Lancashire needed five runs from the final over against Surrey... Allott decided to complete the job with one blow. Which he did, high into the ecstatic crowd behind the bowler...

The NATWEST T20 BLAST

Lancashire finally won this in 2015 after so many near misses.

We thought it would never happen...

DAYS AT THE TEST

'Washbrook, Statham, Tattersall,
England Legends, one and all.'

On the next few pages, are a few cartoons commemorating some of England's better days against our oldest foe. And some of the worst. And some against other countries, at Old Trafford and elsewhere.

DICK POLLARD was a key man in Lancashire's 1934 Championship winning team and was still opening the bowling for Lancashire and for England after the war.. Dick got Bradman out twice in the 1948 Tests - no easy feat..

The next cartoon shows a rare day of toil for the WEST INDIES in 1950. They made England pay for this later in the series. It was a double agony for England followers - we had to listen to that dreadful cricket calypso over and over again..

INDIA have always had talented cricketers, but as a team were not always as successful as they are now. The following cartoon remembers a day at Old Trafford in 1952 when Trueman had the Indian batsmen retreating towards square leg...

THIRD TEST

THE ENTERTAINMENT CAME EARLY TO OLD TRAFFORD ON SATURDAY

HAS IT STARTED? HAVE I MISSED ANYTHING THEN?

EVANS ENJOYED HIMSELF MOST.

I WISH I COULD BE IN T'STANDS WATCHING THIS...

WHEN EVANS WAS OUT, ENGLAND DECLARED. TRUEMAN WAS GUTTED. HE'D BOUGHT A NEW BAT AND COULDN'T USE IT.

LET ME GET AT 'EM

WE'VE DECLARED, FRED...

HE WAS SO CROSS HE WENT OUT AND GOT **EIGHT** WICKETS IN NO TIME, AND WITHOUT EVEN CHANGING HIS SOCKS HE WAS AT IT AGAIN...

UMRIGAR DIDN'T FANCY FRED AT ALL, HE WAS BEHIND THE SQUARE LEG UMPIRE WHEN HE WAS BOWLED,

IT'S NOT PRETTY, POLLY.

IF WE'D SEEN ANY MORE OF THEIR OPENING BAT, WE STILL WOULDN'T HAVE SEEN MUCH, HE COLLECTED A PAIR. QUICKLY.

HOW DID YOU GET ON, BRIEFLY?

BLINDFOLD?

INDIA WERE BOWLED OUT TWICE IN A TRICE, IT WAS LIKE WALKING DAY IN WIGAN.

There's a sketch of the day Willie Watson and Trevor Bailey denied Australia on that famous last day at Lord's. If England had lost that one there's no way the Ashes could have been won back in 1953.

This was England's second Test Match of the very hot summer of 1955, at Lord's, when BRIAN STATHAM blew away South Africa's batsmen in their second innings. 'George' was at the peak of his career, and proved his fitness in an extremely long spell of bowling, broken only by the luncheon interval.

111 is 'Nelson', of course, and this was the third time in a year that England had bowled out the opposition for that exact score.

At the ripe old age of 41 Lancashire's CYRIL WASHBROOK was persuaded to return to the England team in 1956 to help his country out of a difficult situation.

And two weeks later JIM LAKER did his stuff at Old Trafford, and those Ashes were safe in our possession for another year or two.

NEW ZEALAND have produced some truly great cricketers, some within living memory... Bert Sutcliffe, John Reid, Bev Congdon, Sir Richard Hadlee, Glen Turner, Kane Williamson and Danny Morrison...

Danny Morrison? They say that he watched countless episodes of Coronation Street to familiarise himself with Lancashire life before joining the county in 1992. Was he one of Lancashire's better overseas signings? You, dear reader, must decide.

Remembered here is a snooze fest from a Test in 1958...

Fast medium bowler KEN HIGGS was Mr Reliable for Lancashire and England. And he often did well with the bat, as on this occasion at the Oval in 1966...

THIRD TEST
AT HEADINGLEY...

SO BOB FINISHED OFF YESTERDAY WHAT BEEFY BEGAN ON SATURDAY — ONE INCREDIBLE TEST MATCH TURNAROUND.

SO HERE'S **BOB WILLIS**, **EIGHT** FOR **43**, HIS HAIR SEEMING TO GROW LONGER AND WILDER WITH EVERY AUSSIE WICKET HE TOOK...

AUSTRALIA, WANTING ONLY 130, CRASHED TO **75** FOR **EIGHT**.

HUGHES, YALLOP AND BORDER WERE THREE DUCKS IN A ROW.

IT WAS JUST LIKE HILDA OGDEN'S WALL.

WHEN HE MISHOOKED WILLIS, MARSH'S FACE WAS A PICTURE OF HORROR AS HE WAITED TO SEE IF DILLEY WOULD SPILL THE CATCH.

DILLEY DIDN'T.

BUT WITH THE LAST AUSSIE PAIR TOGETHER, CHRIS OLD DID DROP A COUPLE IN THE SLIPS...

MORE HORROR, ESPECIALLY ON THE FACES OF THE HEADINGLEY SHOOTING GALLERY.

IT DIDN'T MATTER, BOB FINISHED THE JOB WITH A BEAUTIFUL YORKER WHICH BRIGHT WASN'T BRIGHT ENOUGH TO KEEP OUT.

THIS TIME THE HEADS WERE HAPPY.

WILLIS? HE JUST KEPT RUNNING ALL THE WAY TO THE DRESSING ROOM.

Bob Bond

Coming closer to the present day, some of us remember exactly where we were when Beefy played his incredible innings at Headingley. BOB WILLIS completed the job.

SHANE WARNE bowled the ball of the century one day at Old Trafford to dismiss Mike Gatting.

SECOND TEST

THE WATCHING POPULACE AT LORD'S YESTERDAY RESEMBLED A FOOTBALL CROWD.

ONE ALMOST EXPECTED TOILET ROLLS TO BE THROWN, AND RIBALD COMMENTS...

SEND 'IM OFF, UMPIRE!

THERE WAS CAREFUL EXPECTANCY WHILE ATHERTON AND VAUGHAN PROSPERED...

95 1

CAN WE PLAY YOU EVERY WEEK?

160 8

DISMAY AS ENGLAND FALTERED...

191 8

OH DOMINIC! LET ME KISS YOU!

THEN ABSOLUTE EUPHORIA WHEN CORK STRUCK THE WINNING RUNS.

YOUR PLACE... OR MINE?

PERFECT STRANGERS HUGGED EACH OTHER...

DOES THIS MEAN I'M **NOT** GOING TO BE EJECTED?

STEWARDS LEFT THEIR DUTIES TO RUN ON TO THE FIELD...

SCORECARD SELLERS TOSSED ASIDE THEIR WARES...

HOW DO YOU **FEEL** RIGHT NOW?

TV PUNDITS RACED ACROSS THE SACRED GRASS TO INTERVIEW THE HEROES... AND THE LOSERS.

WITH SIX WICKETS, COURTNEY WALSH DIDN'T DESERVE TO FINISH ON THE LOSING SIDE.

HIS GLARE ALONE WOULD HAVE WITHERED LESSER OPPOSITION.

BUT NEITHER COURTNEY NOR CURTLY COULD FAZE DARREN GOUGH. UNLIKE RAMPRAKASH WHOSE QUICKSTEP LET HIM DOWN AT THE VITAL MOMENT, GOUGH DANCED FAULTLESSLY.

ARE YOU WATCHING, RAMPS?

DOMINIC CORK, STRICTLY THE REAL HERO OF THE HOUR.

Lord's again, and a close and exciting England win over the West Indies in 2000. A Test all finished in three days...

2005... what a year that was. McGrath's bowling on the very first day...

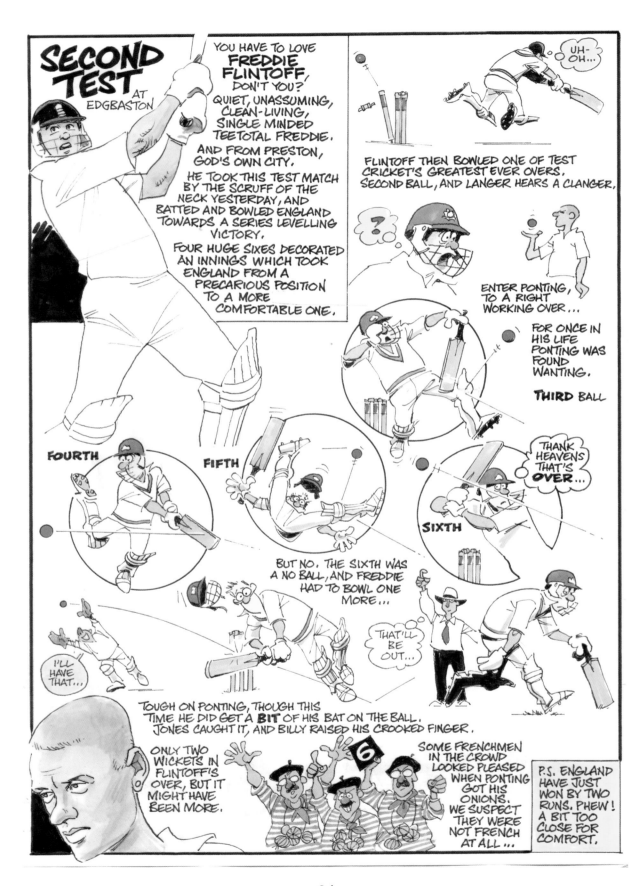

SECOND TEST AT EDGBASTON

YOU HAVE TO LOVE **FREDDIE FLINTOFF**, DON'T YOU? QUIET, UNASSUMING, CLEAN-LIVING, SINGLE MINDED TEETOTAL FREDDIE. AND FROM PRESTON, GOD'S OWN CITY.

HE TOOK THIS TEST MATCH BY THE SCRUFF OF THE NECK YESTERDAY, AND BATTED AND BOWLED ENGLAND TOWARDS A SERIES LEVELLING VICTORY.

FOUR HUGE SIXES DECORATED AN INNINGS WHICH TOOK ENGLAND FROM A PRECARIOUS POSITION TO A MORE COMFORTABLE ONE.

UH-OH...

FLINTOFF THEN BOWLED ONE OF TEST CRICKET'S GREATEST EVER OVERS, SECOND BALL, AND LANGER HEARS A CLANGER.

?

ENTER PONTING, TO A RIGHT WORKING OVER...

FOR ONCE IN HIS LIFE PONTING WAS FOUND WANTING.

THIRD BALL

THANK HEAVENS THAT'S **OVER**...

FOURTH

FIFTH

SIXTH

BUT NO, THE SIXTH WAS A NO BALL, AND FREDDIE HAD TO BOWL ONE MORE...

I'LL HAVE THAT...

THAT'LL BE OUT...

TOUGH ON PONTING, THOUGH THIS TIME HE DID GET A **BIT** OF HIS BAT ON THE BALL. JONES CAUGHT IT, AND BILLY RAISED HIS CROOKED FINGER.

ONLY TWO WICKETS IN FLINTOFF'S OVER, BUT IT MIGHT HAVE BEEN MORE.

SOME FRENCHMEN IN THE CROWD LOOKED PLEASED WHEN PONTING GOT HIS ONIONS. WE SUSPECT THEY WERE NOT FRENCH AT ALL...

P.S. ENGLAND HAVE JUST WON BY TWO RUNS. PHEW! A BIT TOO CLOSE FOR COMFORT.

And then Freddie's astonishing over at Edgbaston. Just a couple of highlights from an unforgettable series.

You simply have to love JIMMY ANDERSON, don't you? Even as these adoring lines are being writ, Jimmy is still running in for England, as keen as ever to improve on his already large haul of Test Match wickets. But don't you just wish that he would put away his England cap and sweater and retire gracefully from the Test arena? And then give three or four years to the Lancashire cause alone? Only then could he go back to his farm in Burnley and be remembered as a true Lancashire legend, safe in the knowledge that he had given his all in the service of his country and his county.

Here is one of his match winning performances for England...

LANCASHIRE LEGENDS

'Although the mould He always breaks
Great cricketers God sometimes makes.'

Sydney, 1894...

Australia, wanting only 177 to win, closed the fourth day on 113 for two. Easy progress towards victory in the morning, then. JOHNNY BRIGGS of Lancashire and Yorkshire's Bobby Peel, having slept soundly and not heard the rain, went out to look at the wicket the next morning...

'Eh Johnny – somebody's bin peeing on this in t'neet...'
'We shall 'ave 'em out in no time, Bobby...'

They did, too. England won by ten runs. Briggs took a lot of wickets for Lancashire with his left arm spin.

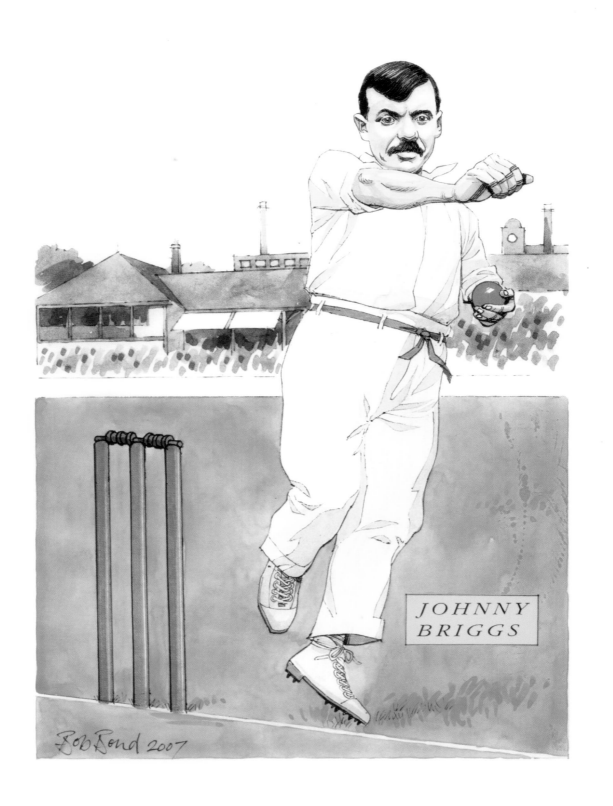

JOHNNY BRIGGS

Bob Bond 2007

ARCHIE
MacLAREN

Bob Bond 2007

By all accounts ARCHIE MacLAREN was a majestic cricketer. He captained and commanded both Lancashire and England in the 1890s and in the early years of the twentieth century. He made what is still the highest individual score for Lancashire. He plucked Sidney Barnes from the relative obscurity of League cricket and took him to Australia with his 1901-02 team, where Barnes was an immediate success. MacLaren was a classic strokemaker all around the wicket. In the field he directed his bowlers and fieldsmen with the same discipline.

The England team that he led is still considered as the best ever, and included JT TYLDESLEY, Lancashire's supreme batsman, affectionately known as 'John Tommy'. His great innings for his country was on a vile pitch at Melbourne in 1904, when all around him were helpless. JT stayed until an England victory was secure. Both MacLaren and Tyldesley were in a great Lancashire side that won the County Championship in 1904.

JOHN THOMAS
TYLDESLEY

ERNEST
TYLDESLEY

ERNEST TYLDESLEY took over as Lancashire's leading batsman where his elder brother left off. He was not an automatic choice for England, as JT was. But one year Ernest was in such prolific form for the county that the selectors simply could not ignore him.

'We want Tyldesley,
We want Tyldesley,
We want Tyldesley...
Tyldesley for the Test!'

Think 2005, and the fanaticism there was for the Old Trafford Test. Now go to 1926 and find almost the same enthusiasm as England tried to win back the Ashes after a long time without them. No, the lyrics were not very inventive, but the Lancashire faithful were very keen to see their own man doing his bit for his country. So such hero worship is nothing new. They got their request - Ernest played - top scored for England - and was instantly dropped. He had been knocked out and bowled out by the same ball by Ernie Gregory on his previous encounter with the Aussies five years earlier.

One day in the early 1930s Nottinghamshire were the visitors to Old Trafford, and Harold Larwood 'practiced' his bodyline attack on Lancashire's unsuspecting batsmen. The following day TED McDONALD, steaming with a feeling of revenge, entered the opponents dressing room.

'I'm telling you lot to ring up hospital down the road and make arrangements for stretchers and ambulances and beds...'

TED
McDONALD

GEORGE
DUCKWORTH

Bob Bond 2007

'Will you end this constant appealing? It's like umpiring in a parrot house!' Alex Skelding is reputed to have said, as he officiated in a Roses match between the wars. GEORGE DUCKWORTH was possibly the worst offender. All but the very firmest umpires must have been intimidated by his screeching claims. George was Lancashire's wicketkeeper during their successful Championship winning years, and good enough to play for England. On retiring from playing, he became their baggage carrier when they went on tour, and broadcast intelligently on Rugby League as well as cricket.

It's part of cricket legend how EDDIE PAYNTER discharged himself from a sick bed in a Brisbane hospital to rescue an ailing England and turn a losing position into a winning one. This was during the Bodyline Tests of 1932-33. Captain Douglas Jardine was not over impressed with Paynter's stoicism.

'Didn't that army march on Kandahar with the fever on them?'

EDDIE PAYNTER

BobBond 2007

CYRIL
WASHBROOK

'Nice one Cyril! Nice one son...
Nice one Cyril – let's have another one!'

No, the song was not about CYRIL WASHBROOK, but it could have been. On the attack, Washbrook was thrilling to watch, having all the shots in the book. Best of all was a crunching square cut which knocked the whitewash off many a ringside fence. His cover fielding was electric, and he ran out many a batsman looking to steal a sharp single. Nice one, Cyril...

Off spinner ROY TATTERSALL took hundreds of wickets for Lancashire after the Second World War. 1950 was his great year when he topped the country's averages with nearly 200 wickets. The following year he bowled England to victory against South Africa at Lord's, with twelve wickets in the match.

FAROKH ENGINEER

The charming FAROKH ENGINEER came to play for Lancashire in 1968, arriving like a breath of fresh air. For India he'd already taken apart a fearsome West Indian attack in Madras with what was almost a century before lunch. That was how exciting his batting could be, and his wicketkeeping was equally dazzling. So he brought so much pleasure to his colleagues and to spectators alike. Early in this book there's a page celebrating a typical all-round Sunday League performance by Farokh. He continued to play for Lancashire until 1976, helping them to all of their early one day successes.

NEIL FAIRBROTHER also served his county and country well on the cricket field. He may have underachieved at Test Match level, but no one could deny his work in one-day internationals, beginning with his breakthrough innings against the West Indies in 1991. That was at Lord's, where he was also a part of many of Lancashire's triumphant limited overs finals.

NEIL FAIRBROTHER
Lord's 1991

ANDREW
FLINTOFF

Enough has been written about ANDREW FLINTOFF's contribution to Lancashire and England, and somewhere else in this book is a cartoon commentary of his legendary over at Edgbaston against Australia in 2005. Was the fabled Prestonian not deserving of an open-top bus tour all to himself through his own city centre?

OLD TRAFFORD

A potted history

'Where lady streakers never run
Across the pitch to spoil the fun.'

But what would L S Lowry have made of the Old Trafford cricket scene? Did he ever sit in the opposite stand and gaze across at the red brick pavilion and wonder how he would fit his matchstick men into such a majestic picture? No, he didn't. But if he had, would it have looked something like this?

And is Old Trafford's reputation for rain completely fair? We know, too, that fog did stop play on one occasion in 1886...

The present pavilion was opened in 1894.

Neville Cardus, the doyen of all cricket writers, made his first appearance in the Old Trafford press box in 1920.

Somerset were beaten in ONE DAY here in 1925.

46,000 people squeezed into the Old Trafford ground on the
August Bank Holiday in 1926 to see the Roses Match.

England's Test Match was completely rained off here in 1938.
Neither they nor Australia bowled a single ball on any of the five days.

All the cricketing giants passed through this gate, on their way out to bat or to field. Bradman, Hobbs, Hutton, Woolley... as well as the saintly Winston Place. Neil Harvey went through the gate to make a century in the Test Match in 1953. In 1956 against England he entered and exited twice in one day, with a couple of ducks.

Of all the drawings in this book this may have been the first to be done... The Old Trafford scoreboard, at the end of the first day's play in a Test Match. The real anoraks out there would know exactly when this was.

And did this conversation take place in 1956?
England official: *'Can you prepare a wicket that will take spin on the second day?'*
Bert Flack: *'I'll see what I can do...'*

Even though he was sitting side on to the wicket, giving lbws was easy. The section of the crowd perched under the pavilion clock became known as the PIT OF HATE. Opinionated, fiercely Lancashire, their hatred was mainly directed at any opposition player or umpire who they didn't agree with. They could easily turn on their own men, too. It was football in a cricket setting...

In recent years funeral services have taken place here, with grieving relatives spreading the ashes of their loved one across the Old Trafford outfield... And LADIES were finally allowed into the sacred pavilion.

LANCASHIRE

A miscellany

'One of the finest sights in cricket
Was Makepeace, on a sticky wicket.'

DICK BARLOW and ALBERT HORNBY were immortalised in the famous poem, of course. Barlow was the slowcoach of the two, and once batted through a whole innings for five not out...

Barlow was equally famous as an umpire when his playing career ended, and also as a soccer referee. In charge of an FA Cup tie between Preston North End and Hyde United, he allowed a North End goal which was clearly offside. It may have been a critical decision. Preston were only 19 goals ahead at the time, on the way to a 26-0 victory.

ALLAN STEEL was the first Lancashire superstar. In the 1878 Roses match at Old Trafford he took 14 Yorkshire wickets for 112.

The Rev. VERNON ROYLE was the Clive Lloyd of his day - a superb fieldsman. He was known as 'The Policeman' and patrolled the covers for Lancashire, deterring batsmen from any thoughts of stealing a quick single...

George Ulyett was for Yorkshire, not Lancashire, but had an important bit part in Old Trafford folklore. It was George who thought he could end a bitterly fought Roses match with one mighty blow. A sixer, and Yorkshire would win by one wicket. Luckily for Lancashire and unluckily for Yorkshire his hit had more height than length, and fell into the bucket hands of ALBERT WARD, standing on the boundary edge. So the red rose, not the white, won the day...

ARTHUR MOLD took hundreds of wickets for
Lancashire, but his career was ended when notorious umpire
Jim Phillips no-balled him for throwing in 1901.

WILLIS CUTTELL was a fast bowler with a bushy growth on his
top lip (see also 'Moustaches'). He pre-dated Brearley, but also had a
particular dislike of cricketing clergymen.
*'Look behind you, Reverend – I think I made a mess of your b****y pulpit..'*

WALTER BREARLEY would bowl fast all day if he was asked to, and usually did. Even when he wasn't asked to. Even when his face was as red as a beetroot and he was sweating like a horse, he was a hard man to tell to have a rest...

McLaren (captain) *'I think it's time for a change, Walter...'*

Brearley. *'Aye Archie, I'll 'ave a go from other end...'*

When Albert Knight of Leicestershire (and England) used to pray when he came out to bat, Brearley thought it entirely unfair and an unequal contest. Also, Brearley remarked, it was contrary to all the laws of cricket, if not the laws of the universe..'

Great bowler as he was, he rarely troubled the scorers when batting. It was said that at the sight of Brearley going out to bat, the horse would back into the shafts ready to roll the wicket.

REGGIE SPOONER, son of a Vicar, made his Test debut in 1905. He wouldn't have felt lonely because three other Lancastrians were in the same England team. It was in this series that the Australian captain, Joe Darling, lost the toss in all of the first four Tests. Before going out to toss for the Fifth Test, Joe did twenty press-ups and stripped to the waist. To no avail - he lost the toss again. Spooner and John Tyldesley put on 158 runs for the sixth England wicket.

Some batsmen's defences are like a jar with a stiff lid. HARRY MAKEPEACE was such a stubborn opener. No fours before lunch, on principle. Then he could, if the occasion demanded, bat freely and attractively. Harry worked faithfully for Lancashire as player and then as coach.

JACK SHARP served Lancashire faithfully for many years, some as captain. It was unfair, then, that he should be cruelly barracked one morning at Old Trafford for dropping a simple catch. Disappointed, Sharp threatened never to play there again, although he later relented. Like Makepeace, he played soccer for Everton.

CECIL PARKIN was the joker in a pack of serious Lancashire men.
'Trumper? Why, I could have bowled him out with an orange...'
His teammates didn't always see the joke. *'I'll have none of that kind of talk, Parkin, if you don't mind.'* The frosty response was from Ted McDonald, a fellow countryman of Trumper. *'Wait a minute, Ted – he were only jokin'...'*

An enormously talented bowler, he took 14 wickets in one match in helping Lancashire to beat Yorkshire in 1919. Parkin enjoyed the game more than any other cricketer of his time. He challenged authority, and that was his downfall. At Old Trafford in 1924 the rotund DICK TYLDESLEY took FIVE Leicestershire wickets for no runs.

In 1928 FRANK WATSON made 300 not out against Surrey - at that time the highest score to be made at Old Trafford.

In 1930 Lancashire won the County Championship for the fourth time in five years, with probably their best-ever team.

When PETER ECKERSLEY led Lancashire to their County Championship win in 1934, he would not have guessed it would be 77 years before they won it again outright. Yorkshire maintained that if FOUR of their best players had not been required by England in defence of the Ashes that summer, the title would definitely have been won by them and not Lancashire. 'Would it eckerslike!' replied Eckersley.

BLACKPOOL! We love the seaside town that gave us golden sands, donkey rides, the Tower and its Ballroom, its Circus and Charlie Cairoli, the Golden Mile, the Illuminations, three Piers, Stanley Matthews, fish and chips, and Billy's Weekly Liar. And cricket... here's Lancashire at Blackpool in 1952. To see who they played that week, you'll have to consult Wisden.

In that team, as you can see, was KEN GRIEVES. He was not the first Australian to play for Lancashire, but he was one of the most popular. A prolific run scorer and a useful spin bowler, Grieves was also a sensational close catcher, throwing himself around like a goalkeeper... which he was, of course, in his winter job with Bolton Wanderers, Bury and Stockport County.

When MALCOLM HILTON dismissed Don Bradman TWICE in the Australian Tourists' match against Lancashire in 1948, there were immediate calls for him to be chosen to play for England, presumably in the sure and certain hope that he would easily topple the great man twice more! Hilton was invited to attend a Crazy Gang show in London where, on stage, a conjuror produced from his pockets two live rabbits. One he called 'Don' and the other he called 'Bradman'.
'Hilton's rabbits!' said the conjuror...

When JACK IKIN caught Don Bradman off Bill Voce in the first Ashes Test at Brisbane in 1946, all England knew that they had the prize wicket. Bradman stood his ground, and amazingly the umpire didn't give him out, thinking that it could possibly have been a bump ball as it left Bradman's bat. To his dying day, Ikin was convinced it was a clean catch. Bradman went on to make one of his huge scores, and England were later caught on a notorious Brisbane sticky dog, and lost heavily.

After he had taken his ten wickets against Australia, and England had completed their victory, JIM LAKER drove home alone. Calling at a convenient hostelry, BBC Television were replaying highlights of his achievement. Nobody noticed or recognised Jim as he entered the pub. He left incognito...

Brian Statham training for the forthcoming season...

Wicketkeeper GEOFF CLAYTON was his own man. Trouble followed him around like a faithful hound. On one occasion he walked into the dressing room with a black eye. Why? Nobody found out... He lost favour with Lancashire when he put up the shutters in a one-day game as a protest against a deep set field. That signalled the end of his tenure at Old Trafford.

In the days of dour, attritional cricket, spectators loved someone who could give it a 'bit of welly'. ROY COLLINS was such a man. His career was not long enough.

PETER MARNER once drove Leicestershire's Jack Savage clean over Stand H - one of the truly great hits at Old Trafford. Marner, a rugger player too, was thrilling to watch in full flow. He later played for Leicestershire, while Savage made the opposite transfer.

It's generally believed that GEOFF PULLAR was always 'Noddy' because he was able to fall asleep anywhere. Or perhaps it was because he drove an open-top car like Enid Blyton's Noddy.

He never slept when he was batting. He became the first Lancashire batsman to score a Test century at Old Trafford against India in 1959. Pullar hit three hundreds against Yorkshire in one season, which endeared him to Lancashire followers even more.

On leaving Lancashire, where he was mainly slow and stern-faced, BOB BARBER blossomed into a flashing, destructive opening batsman for Warwickshire and England.

Leg spinner TOMMY GREENHOUGH and opening batsman DAVID GREEN were both popular players during Lancashire's relatively barren years of the 1960s.

Before playing for Lancashire, FAROKH ENGINEER had played against them in a friendly match at Southport. He hit one of the Lancashire bowlers on to the railway line! Not until afterwards did he learn that the bowler was none other than Brian Statham...

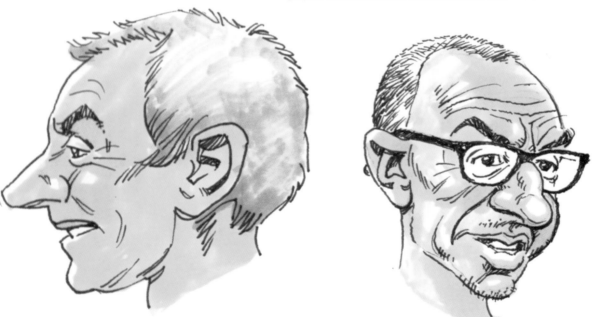

We all laughed at the Bumblies, didn't we? Those of us who are old enough to remember them, anyway. Cute little extra-terrestrials from the planet Bumble, they were befriended by an absent minded professor (Michael Bentine) in whose garden their spacecraft had crash landed. The Bumblies had noses that were... long. Quite why DAVID LLOYD should become 'Bumble' is a mystery. Lloyd captained Lancashire to their fourth Gillette Cup win in 1974, later did a stint of first class umpiring, and then became one of our best loved cricket commentators.

Once, on an 'away' ground, as Clive and David were resuming their innings after an interval, this announcement was heard...

'Do not adjust your set - he really is that wide...' At the hugely reassuring sight of JACK SIMMONS coming out to bat, David Lloyd was doing the television commentary. Maybe it was his liking for fish and chips that contributed to Jack's wideness. Fittingly the chip shop was called 'Jack's', as if he were its only customer.

'Not out!?' Complained Jack on another occasion. 'Not out? It would have knocked down all three 'Maybe...' said umpire Dickie Bird. 'But I couldn't give him 'cos couldn't see past you...' Harry Pilling and Jack Simmons doing their roadwork prior to a new season..

Fast medium bowler PETER LEE gave great service to Lancashire in the 1970s. Twice he was the country's leading wicket taker in the County Championship,with over a hundred wickets each time. 'Just one more over, Peter?'skipper David Lloyd would ask. Lee was untiring. He also sported a wonderful moustache. This is the place, then, to celebrate some of the wonderful MOUSTACHES on Lancashire players down the years, especially in the early days. Here are a few...

BARRY WOOD just missed a Test Match hundred on his England debut in 1970.

FRANK HAYES did great things for Lancashire, but was unlucky in that all his Test appearances were against the West Indies and their fearsome quartet of fast bowlers. After a century in his first England Test, it was hard going for Frank. But he so nearly equalled Sobers's maximum when he struck 34 runs from one over. Also from Glamorgan's Malcolm Nash! He was known as 'Fish' by his colleagues, possibly a reference to his drinking capacity....

GRAEME FOWLER is spoken of with affection around Southport following his two centuries in Lancashire's incredible defeat of Warwickshire in 1982 - with someone else running all of his runs for him. 'Foxy' was also good enough to score a double century for England.

And HAIRCUTS... The prize for the best Afro to be on show at Old Trafford must go to Bernard Reidy. Bob Arrowsmith (another of the great Bobs) had an excellent curly perm, clearly influenced by Kevin Keegan. John Abrahams was given the Man of the Match award in the Benson and Hedges Cup final in 1984, presumably for having the best barnet. It was certainly not for having the most runs.

'Gel is more macho than a hair band' said Wasim Akram, who had more hair than most to keep under control. Sometimes he looked as if he'd had it cut with a knife and fork.

Here are a few impressions of WEST INDIAN cricketers who have played for Lancashire, with varying degrees of success... Clive Lloyd, Patrick Patterson, Colin Croft, Sonny Ramadhin and Michael Holding.

A local radio station hailed Warwickshire as County Champions in 2011. BEFORE the last day of their match against Hampshire, a match they appeared certain to win. They didn't win. Later in the day Lancashire were crowned Champions.

MORE OF CRICKET'S DRAMATIC MOMENTS

'Often, with well-matched opponents
Come those memorable moments...'

These little drawings first appeared almost 50 years ago in the Cricketer magazine. I had to be reminded about them. This is simply a selection - there were many more. Nearly everything was in black and white in those days. It was a different kind of drawing... less of a cartoon, more of a picture-strip.

The features were done under two headings. 'The FIGHT FOR THE ASHES' was a potted history of England against Australia, starting with the very first Test Match in Melbourne and ending with Richie Benaud bowling his team to victory on the last afternoon in Manchester in 1961. Remember that?

These stories include a fateful dropped catch, also at Old Trafford, and a catch that was taken, brilliantly, by a substitute fielder. It turned the match England's way (shades of Gary Pratt in 2005). Also here are some episodes from the infamous Bodyline series, including Eddie Paynter rising from his sick bed in Brisbane...

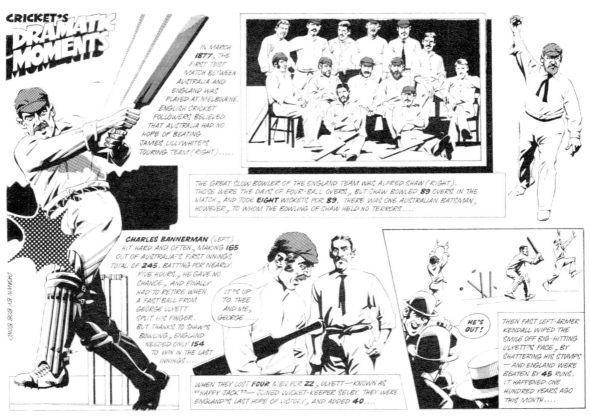

THE FIGHT FOR THE "ASHES"

THE FIRST FOUR TESTS HAD BEEN DRAWN WHEN THE OLD ENEMIES CAME TO THE OVAL IN 1926.... OF ALL THE MEMORABLE PARTNERSHIPS BETWEEN JACK HOBBS AND HERBERT SUTCLIFFE, THIS WAS PROBABLY THE FINEST. THEY BEGAN ENGLAND'S SECOND INNINGS WITH A STAND OF 172, MADE FOR THE MOST PART ON A SPITEFUL PITCH. HOBBS WAS OUT FOR 100, WHILST SUTCLIFFE WENT ON TO REACH 161....

NEEDING TO SCORE 415 TO WIN, AUSTRALIA WERE SOON IN TROUBLE. WOODFULL FLASHED AT LARWOOD....

WELL CAUGHT!

ENGLAND HAD RECALLED WILFRED RHODES, AT THE AGE OF 48, TO PLAY IN THIS VITAL MATCH

BOWLING WITH ALL HIS OLD SKILL AND CUNNING, RHODES SOON BEGAN TO PICK UP WICKETS.... PONSFORD, COLLINS AND BARDSLEY ALL CAUGHT IN THE SLIPS, AND RICHARDSON BOWLED, NECK AND CROP.

WHEN GEORGE GEARY TRIMMED THE BAILS OFF ARTHUR MAILEY'S WICKET, ENGLAND HAD WON A GREAT VICTORY, BY 289 RUNS, AND THE CROWD SWARMED IN FRONT OF THE PAVILION TO CHEER THEIR HEROES. THE ASHES HAD RETURNED, AFTER FOURTEEN YEARS....

ENGLAND!

CRICKET'S DRAMATIC MOMENTS

THE FIRST TEST, AT TRENT BRIDGE, IN 1930.... ENGLAND ENDED THEIR SECOND INNINGS WITH A LEAD OF 428 OVER AUSTRALIA, BUT HERBERT SUTCLIFFE, IN MAKING 58, HAD INJURED A HAND...

IT'S BAD, SKIPPER, I'M SORRY, BUT I WON'T BE ABLE TO FIELD...

DON'T WORRY — I'LL LOOK AROUND FOR A SUBSTITUTE.

A YOUNG MAN FROM THE TRENT BRIDGE GROUND STAFF WALKED OUT TO FIELD ON THE LAST DAY, WITH THE BEST OF ENGLAND'S CRICKETERS! SOON DON BRADMAN (RIGHT) REACHED HIS FIRST TEST HUNDRED IN ENGLAND....

CRACKK!

AT 229 FOR THREE, AUSTRALIA WERE IN A WINNING POSITION. ONLY 200 MORE WERE NEEDED, AND BRADMAN'S PARTNERSHIP WITH STAN McCABE WAS LOOKING OMINOUS. THEN McCABE DROVE POWERFULLY (ABOVE) AT MAURICE TATE....

MID-ON DIVED SIDEWAYS, THREW OUT A HAND, AND HELD UP THE BALL TRIUMPHANTLY! IT WAS COPLEY, THE UNKNOWN SUBSTITUTE, WHO HAD TAKEN THIS ASTONISHING CATCH!

McCABE WAS OUT FOR 49, AND, BRADMAN FOLLOWING SOON, ENGLAND WON EASILY...

STAN McCABE (ABOVE) WENT ON TO PLAY TWO OF THE MOST BRILLIANT TEST INNINGS AGAINST ENGLAND, BUT COPLEY WAS NEVER HEARD OF AGAIN.

THE FIGHT FOR THE "ASHES"

1961... EACH SIDE HAD WON ONE MATCH WHEN THEY ARRIVED AT OLD TRAFFORD FOR THE FOURTH TEST. NINE WICKETS DOWN IN THEIR SECOND INNINGS, AUSTRALIA LED BY ONLY **157**.... BUT PEOPLE WATCHED DISMAYED, ON THE GROUND AND AT HOME, AS A STUBBORN LAST WICKET STAND SWUNG THE MATCH....

ANOTHER FOUR TO DAVIDSON... HE AND McKENZIE HAVE ADDED OVER EIGHTY!

IN FACT, AUSTRALIA'S LAST PAIR PUT ON **98** BEFORE McKENZIE HAD HIS STUMPS WRECKED. EVEN SO, ENGLAND'S TARGET OF **256** IN **230** MINUTES LOOKED TO BE WELL WITHIN REACH WHEN TED DEXTER MOVED INTO TOP GEAR (LEFT).

A SUCCESSION OF MAJESTIC STROKES TOOK ENGLAND TO **150** FOR ONE WICKET — AHEAD OF THE CLOCK, TOO.... THE SPECTATORS CHEERED EVERY STROKE, HAPPILY, **RICHIE BENAUD** (LEFT), DEXTER'S RIVAL SKIPPER AND A SUPERB SPINNER, COULD HARDLY STEM THE FLOW OF RUNS....

SUDDENLY, DEXTER CUT AT BENAUD ONCE TOO OFTEN, AND WAS CAUGHT BEHIND. WITH **76** TO HIS NAME IN **82** MINUTES, HE RETURNED TO TREMENDOUS APPLAUSE.

WELL BATTED, TED!

BUT WITH HIS DISMISSAL, HAD ENGLAND'S CHANCE ALSO GONE?

THE GREAT PETER MAY WENT NEXT, BOWLED ROUND HIS LEGS.... FOR **0**.

IF THEY WERE WINNING A SHORT TIME BEFORE, NOW ENGLAND WERE STRUGGLING. BOWLING INTELLIGENTLY AND TURNING HIS LEG-BREAKS SHARPLY, BENAUD FINISHED WITH **SIX** WICKETS FOR **70**. WHEN DAVIDSON BOWLED STATHAM, AUSTRALIA HAD WON THE MATCH AND RETAINED THE "ASHES"....

The other heading was CRICKET'S DRAMATIC MOMENTS, of which only the six sixes in one over, struck by Gary Sobers, and one or two others, would be within living memory.

We can only wish we could have been there when Trott drove the ball over the pavilion at Lord's, and when Hobbs got his record-breaking century. And when Sutcliffe and Holmes achieved another record with their huge opening partnership. If only we'd been at Hove to witness Alletson's innings... And...

CRICKET'S DRAMATIC MOMENTS

DISTANCE FROM FAR WICKET TO BACK OF PAVILION — OVER **120 YARDS**

THE PAVILION AT LORD'S — THE BEST-KNOWN EDIFICE IN CRICKET, ALTHOUGH THE GAME HAS KNOWN SOME IMMENSE HITTERS OF A BALL — THORNTON, BONNOR, CRAWFORD, MANN, WELLARD, JIM SMITH, CLIVE LLOYD — STILL ONLY ONE MAN HAS EVER STRUCK THE BALL **OVER** THIS FAMOUS LANDMARK. HE WAS **ALBERT TROTT**, OF AUSTRALIA AND MIDDLESEX, WHO MADE HIS GREAT HIT ON THE LAST DAY OF JULY, **1899**.....

STRANGE TO RELATE, TROTT (RIGHT) HAD MADE A BIGGER HIT A FEW WEEKS EARLIER, OFF FRED TATE OF SUSSEX, WHICH STRUCK THE EMBLEM ON THE PINNACLE OF ONE OF THE TOWERS OF THE LORD'S PAVILION. THIS HIT LEFT TROTT DISSATISFIED....

TROTT LATER RECALLED HIS **GREAT HIT**...

IT WAS DURING AN INNINGS OF **41** FOR MCC AGAINST THE AUSTRALIAN TOURING TEAM....

TROTT GRINNED HUGELY AS HE SAW HIS DRIVE, OFF THE BOWLING OF FELLOW-AUSTRALIAN MONTY NOBLE, DISAPPEAR OVER THE TOP....

IT'S GONE... **RIGHT OVER!**

WELL MIGHT THE SPECTATORS GASP — IF IT WASN'T THE BIGGEST HIT EVER MADE AT LORD'S, IT CERTAINLY WAS THE MOST FAMOUS, AND HAS YET TO BE EQUALLED....

DRAWN BY BOB BOND

CRICKET'S DRAMATIC MOMENTS

TED ALLETSON BECAME A CRICKET IMMORTAL BECAUSE OF A SINGLE INNINGS — SURELY THE MOST REMARKABLE INNINGS **EVER** PLAYED....

20TH. MAY 1911.... IT WAS THE LAST DAY OF THE MATCH BETWEEN SUSSEX AND NOTTINGHAMSHIRE AT HOVE, AND FIFTY MINUTES BEFORE LUNCH.... **176** RUNS BEHIND ON THE FIRST INNINGS, NOTTS WERE **185** FOR SEVEN IN THEIR SECOND — ONLY NINE RUNS AHEAD — WHEN ALLETSON WENT OUT TO BAT. THEIR SKIPPER, A. O. JONES, HAD GIVEN UP THE GAME AS **LOST**...

PLAY JUST AS YOU LIKE, TED — IT ISN'T GOING TO MATTER...

THEN I'LL GIVE THE BLIGHTERS SOME STICK...

DRAWN BY BOB BOND

IF HE GOES ON MUCH LONGER MY PENCIL'S GONNA CATCH FIRE.....

THE LAST NOTTS WICKET PUT ON **152** AFTER LUNCH, AND ALLETSON (LEFT) MADE ALL BUT TEN OF THEM. HE HIT EIGHT SIXES, MOST OF THEM OUT OF THE GROUND, AND FROM ONE OVER BY ERNIE KILLICK, WHICH HAD TWO NO-BALLS, HE PLUNDERED **34** RUNS. FROM BEING IN A HOPELESS POSITION WHEN HE WENT IN, NOTTS ALMOST WON, FOR SUSSEX HAD EIGHT WICKETS DOWN WHEN THE MATCH WAS LEFT DRAWN. EDWARD BOALER ALLETSON NEVER HIT ANOTHER HUNDRED, BUT WILL ALWAYS BE REMEMBERED FOR THE ONE INCREDIBLE INNINGS HE **DID** PLAY....

MARVELLOUS! I THINK I'LL PAY AGAIN ON THE WAY OUT.....

ALLETSON **DID** GIVE THE SUSSEX BOWLERS SOME STICK... AFTER MAKING **47** BEFORE LUNCH, HE ADDED **142** IN **40** MINUTES FOLLOWING THE INTERVAL — AN AMAZING **189** IN **90** MINUTES, OUT OF **227** RUNS ADDED!

CRICKET'S DRAMATIC MOMENTS

DRAWN BY BOB BOND

IN AUGUST **1920**, BATTING FOR SURREY AGAINST NORTHAMPTONSHIRE, **PERCY FENDER** STRUCK THE FASTEST FIRST CLASS CENTURY OF ALL TIME..... THE SCORER ENTERED IN HIS BOOK THE TIME OF FENDER'S ARRIVAL AT THE WICKET — ONE MINUTE PAST FOUR O'CLOCK....

IN THE **29** MINUTES BEFORE THE TEA INTERVAL, FENDER PULLED AND DROVE THE NORTHANTS BOWLING WITHOUT MERCY, TAKING HIS SCORE TO **91** NOT OUT....

HE DOESN'T GIVE OUR BOWLERS MUCH ENCOURAGEMENT, THIS FELLOW....

FENDER'S ONSLAUGHT HAD THE CROWD AT NORTHAMPTON OPEN-MOUTHED IN ASTONISHMENT....

FENDER WAS **28** YEARS OLD AT THE TIME, AND THIS WAS HIS LAST MATCH BEFORE TAKING OVER AS CAPTAIN OF SURREY. IN HIS LATER YEARS HE BATTED IN SPECTACLES, AND WITH HIS WAVEY HAIR, BLACK MOUSTACHE AND KNEE-LENGTH SWEATER, FENDER WAS IMMORTALISED BY CARTOONIST TOM WEBSTER...

AS SURREY ALREADY HAD A BIG LEAD, IT HAD BEEN THEIR CAPTAIN'S INTENTION TO DECLARE AT THE TEA INTERVAL, BUT....

I'LL WAIT UNTIL YOU'VE GOT YOUR HUNDRED, PERCY...

FENDER'S PARTNER, BERT PEACH, WAS NEAR TO A DOUBLE-CENTURY, SO TOOK MOST OF THE STRIKE AFTER TEA, EVEN SO, FENDER REACHED **100** IN THE INCREDIBLE TIME OF **35** MINUTES — A RECORD NOT YET BEATEN, ALTHOUGH CHRIS OLD CAME MIGHTY CLOSE....

CRICKET'S DRAMATIC MOMENTS

"YOU ASK US TO BAT FIRST ON THIS BILLIARD-TABLE WICKET? YOU MUST BE CRAZY, LIONEL....." LORD LIONEL TENNYSON HAD WON THE TOSS FOR HAMPSHIRE, AND HIS RIVAL SKIPPER, FREDDIE CALTHORPE, GASPED WHEN HE ASKED WARWICKSHIRE TO TAKE FIRST INNINGS...

THE MATCH WAS AT BIRMINGHAM IN **1922**, IT **WAS** A GOOD WICKET.... CALTHORPE HIMSELF (LEFT) MADE **70**, BUT HIS SIDE WERE ALL OUT FOR **223** — A POOR SCORE, SURELY?

WHEN HAMPSHIRE BATTED ON THE FIRST EVENING, THEY WERE SHOT OUT FOR ONLY **15**! CALTHORPE TOOK **FOUR** FOR **FOUR**, AND ONLY THE GREAT PHILIP MEAD (RIGHT) WITH SIX NOT OUT, HAD NO REASON TO BLUSH, EIGHT MEN WERE OUT WITHOUT SCORING! WITH HAMPSHIRE FOLLOWING ON, MEAD WAS AT THE CREASE AGAIN THAT EVENING!

THE ENGLAND LEFT-HANDER WAS SOON OUT ON THE SECOND DAY. AT **127** FOR FOUR, HAMPSHIRE WERE STILL IN DEEP TROUBLE.... "SUITS ME" SAID CALTHORPE, AS LORD TENNYSON ARRIVED AT THE WICKET, "I'VE PLANNED TO PLAY GOLF TOMORROW!" TENNYSON (LEFT) HIT **45** IN AN HOUR. "YOU'LL BE HERE TOMORROW, SWEATING!" HE TOLD CALTHORPE.

HAMPSHIRE WERE STILL BEHIND WHEN TENNYSON WAS OUT — BUT THEN LEFT-HANDED GEORGE BROWN (LEFT) PLAYED AN INCREDIBLE INNINGS OF **172**, GIVEN SOME WONDERFUL ASSISTANCE BY THE TAIL...

WICKET-KEEPER LIVSEY, **110** NOT OUT, HELPED BROWN TO ADD **177**. HAMPSHIRE REACHED **521**, AND THEIR REMARKABLE RECOVERY WAS COMPLETE WHEN THEY BOWLED OUT WARWICKSHIRE FOR **158**, TO WIN COMFORTABLY BY **155** RUNS....

DRAWN BY BOB BOND

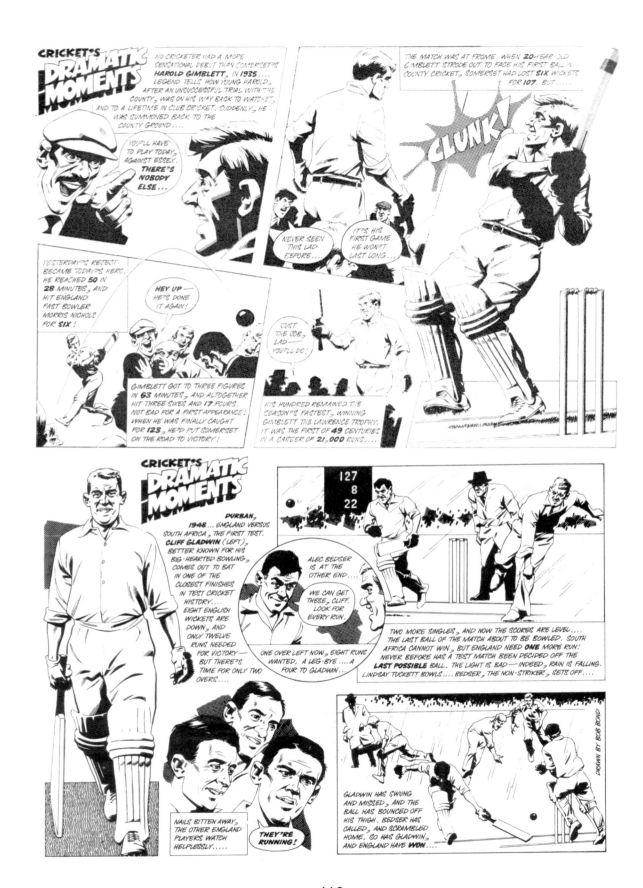

CRICKET'S DRAMATIC MOMENTS

1950.... THE SECOND TEST BETWEEN ENGLAND AND THE WEST INDIES, AT LORD'S....
LEN HUTTON (ON THE LEFT) AND CYRIL WASHBROOK WERE THE BEST OPENING BATSMEN IN ENGLAND. THEY'D TAKEN CENTURIES OFF LINDWALL AND MILLER, AND IN 1948 HAD SET UP A TEST RECORD WITH 359 FOR ENGLAND'S FIRST WICKET AGAINST SOUTH AFRICA. NOW THEY FACED A DIFFERENT THREAT—THE SPIN OF RAMADHIN AND VALENTINE....

DRAWN BY BOB BOND

SONNY RAMADHIN (LEFT) CAPTURED FIVE WICKETS FOR 66 AS ENGLAND TUMBLED FOR 151, AND ALF VALENTINE (RIGHT) FOUR FOR 48. EACH OF THEM HAD PLAYED IN ONLY A HANDFUL OF FIRST-CLASS MATCHES BEFORE THE TOUR, BUT ENGLAND'S BEST BATSMEN WERE BEMUSED. SET 601 TO WIN, IT WAS THE SAME STORY IN THE SECOND INNINGS....

HUTTON HAS BEEN BOWLED BY VALENTINE—NOT OFFERING A STROKE!

WHILE WASHBROOK STAYED, THERE SEEMED TO BE A CHANCE OF SAVING THE GAME. THOUGH UNABLE TO PICK RAMADHIN'S LEG-BREAK FROM HIS OFF-BREAK, WASHBROOK SKILFULLY STUCK TO HIS TASK, AND BATTED THROUGHOUT THE FOURTH DAY.... WHEN RAMADHIN BOWLED HIM FOR 114 ON THE FINAL DAY, THE END WAS NEAR....

ENGLAND LOST BY 326 RUNS, AND THE WEST INDIES WON THE THIRD AND FOURTH TESTS AS WELL, TO TAKE THE SERIES. WEEKES, WORRELL AND WALCOTT MADE RUNS IN STYLE, AND ENGLAND HAD NO ANSWER TO THE SPINNING TWINS.... IT WAS AT LORD'S WHERE THE FAMOUS VICTORY CALYPSO WAS BORN.....

CRICKET, LOVELY CRICKET, AT LORD'S WHERE I SAW IT... THEY GAVE THE CROWD PLENTY FUN, SECOND TEST AND WEST INDIES WON, WITH THOSE TWO LITTLE PALS OF MINE RAMADHIN AND VALENTINE!

CRICKET'S DRAMATIC MOMENTS

ON 31ST AUGUST 1968, AT THE ST. HELEN'S GROUND, SWANSEA, GARFIELD SOBERS ACHIEVED WHAT EVERY CRICKETER HAS DREAMED OF, BUT THOUGHT IMPOSSIBLE.... FROM ONE OVER BY GLAMORGAN'S MALCOLM NASH, ONE OF THE LEADING COUNTY BOWLERS IN THE LAND, SOBERS STRUCK EVERY BALL FOR SIX.....36 RUNS!

DRAWN BY BOB BOND

THAT'S OVER THE TOP AS WELL! I'VE NEVER SEEN ANYTHING LIKE IT...

BUT DOES HE NEED TO DO IT AGAINST GLAMORGAN?

NOTTINGHAMSHIRE WERE 308 FOR FIVE WHEN SOBERS CAME OUT TO BAT, AND NASH HAD TAKEN FOUR OF THE WICKETS. BUT IT WAS THE GLAMORGAN LEFT-ARMER WHO SUFFERED THE RECORD-BREAKING ASSAULT....

HOW DO YOU BOWL TO SOBERS WHEN HE'S IN THIS MOOD?

SOBERS WATCHED ANXIOUSLY AS ROGER DAVIS CAUGHT HIT NUMBER FIVE AT LONG-OFF—BUT IN DOING SO, DAVIS FELL OVER THE BOUNDARY. NOT OUT, AND SIX MORE RUNS!

TWO HITS OVER LONG-OFF

TWO OVER LONG-ON

TWO OVER MID-WICKET

NO DOUBT ABOUT THE LAST HIT—CLEAN OUT OF THE GROUND OVER MID-WICKET, TO BE RETURNED BY A SMALL BOY THE NEXT DAY. A GLAMORGAN MAN, CYRIL SMART, HAD HELD THE RECORD UNTIL THEN—32 RUNS OFF A SIX-BALL OVER, AGAINST HAMPSHIRE AT CARDIFF IN 1935. THEN CAME SOBERS.....

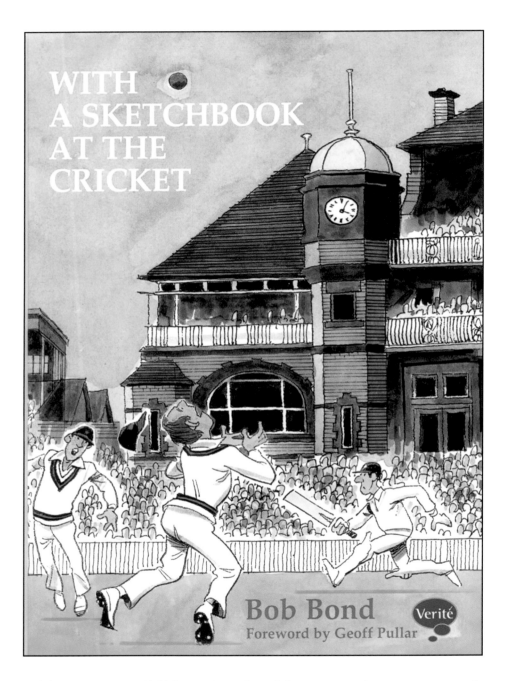

WITH A SKETCHBOOK AT THE CRICKET is a compilation, generously interspersed with drawings, of memories of watching Lancashire andEngland during the 1950s.

THE AUTHOR

WILFRED TATTERSALL AND THE MAN IN BLACK is a fictional, cautionary tale of a cricketer who one day was visited by a mysterious stranger...